Beautiful
Wisconsin

Beautiful
Wisconsin

Concept and Design: Robert D. Shangle
Text: William Curran

First Printing September, 1979
Published by Beautiful America Publishing Company
P.O. Box 608, Beaverton, Oregon 97075
Robert D. Shangle, Publisher

Library of Congress Cataloging in Publication Data
Beautiful Wisconsin
1. Wisconsin—Description and travel—1951- Views. I.
Curran, William, 1921-
F582.B24   917.75'02   79-777
ISBN 0-915796-63-5
ISBN 0-915796-62-7 (paperback)

CONTENTS

Photo Credits

BERT CONGDON—*page 14, above.*

JEFF DEAN—*page 24, below; pages 48-49; page 53, above; page 54.*

KEN DEQUAINE—*page 9; page 10; page 11; pages 12-13; page 14, below; page 15; pages 16-17; page 18; page 19; page 20; page 21; page 22; page 23; page 24, above; page 25; page 28; page 29; pages 32-33; page 36; page 37; page 40; page 41; page 42; pages 44-45; page 46; page 50; page 51; page 52; page 53, below; page 55; page 56; page 57; page 61; pages 64-65; page 68; page 69.*

DAVID MLADENOFF—*page 47, below.*

EUGENE G. SHULZ—*page 47, above.*

RICHARD SMITH—*page 43; page 60.*

DAVE WITMAN—*page 72.*

Enlarged Prints

Most of the photography in this book is available as photographic
enlargements. Send self-addressed, stamped envelope for information.
For a complete product catalog, send $1.00.
Beautiful America Publishing Company
P.O. Box 608
Beaverton, Oregon 97075

CREDITS

Lithography by Fremont Litho Inc., Fremont, California

INTRODUCTION

In 1886 the Reverend David O. Van Slyke, a Methodist minister of Galesville in Trempealeau County, published a pamphlet in which he argued that the countryside drained by the La Crosse, Black and Trempealeau Rivers could be the location of the Biblical Garden of Eden. When one stands on the wooded bluffs of Trempealeau at sunset, under the spell of one of the earth's magnificent river vistas, it is hard not to lend emotional support to Mr. Van Slyke's thesis. It is harder still when one is watching a summer's dawn light up the ''fatness'' of a coulee-country farm.

The preacher's compliment to Wisconsin may be the most extravagant on record, but it doesn't exceed greatly many of the lyrical outbursts from Europeans since they first entered its deep forests and navigated its fast rivers and clear lakes. And who can tell with what intensity the Indian in his oral literature may have celebrated this theme in the centuries before the white man came. By anyone's measure, Wisconsin is a grand place.

Wisconsin was named for the great river that flows diagonally through the state from its source in Lac Vieux Desert on the Upper Michigan border to the Mississippi below Prairie du Chien. The name in its present form was fixed by Presidential order way back in the 1830s, but there never has been universal agreement on what it means or even which Indian language it represents. At any given time, the Wisconsite may have half a dozen translations to choose from, among them ''the stream of the thousand isles,'' ''meeting of the waters,'' or ''the good place.'' Every decade or so a home-grown philologist will put forward a new guess. Such diversity of opinion, like the diversity in its terrain, population, and industries, has characterized Wisconsin's history.

Contrasts, surprises, and paradoxes have long marked the Wisconsin scene. The state license plates identify it as America's Dairyland, a claim well supported by milk and cheese production. In fact, most of Wisconsin's income is from industry—heavy industry. It ranks second among the states in the manufacture of motor vehicles, first in gasoline engines.

Wisconsin is the birthplace of the Republican Party. It is also the first state to send a Socialist to Congress and elect a Socialist mayor of a major city, Milwaukee. The National Forensic Society makes its headquarters in Wisconsin. So does the Burlington Liar's Club. It is the birthplace of the Gideons as well as of the Freethinkers Society.

A Wisconsinite created the round silo and revolutionized animal husbandry; another created the automated assembly line and revolutionized manufacturing. The typewriter was invented in Wisconsin but is not manufactured there.

From Wisconsin minds have sprung the Paul Bunyan legends of rugged individualism and the nation's first workmens' compensation law. It is the cradle of the American traveling circus and also of the "Wisconsin idea," government by academics and specialists. Wisconsin introduced to the nation the county agent, the community theater, and the kindergarten. It challenged the national will power with the creation of malted milk and the ice cream sundae.

There is no static Wisconsin. It is always changing, as active as the yeast in Milwaukee beer. In less than a century, the face of the state has been dramatically altered all the way from the Illinois border to Lake Superior. This is not to say that today's face is less pleasant. True, the forest giants of the North Woods, and the great stands of white pine are lost to us forever. The new, more modest growth—the jack pine and aspen, hemlock, tamarack and cedar, the paper birch and black ash—while they lack the grandeur of the virgin forest, do admit sunshine where none had fallen for centuries. They share the earth with wild flowers, with sweet fern, bracken, blueberries, wild currant, bush honeysuckle and trailing arbutus. All this has its own kind of beauty. As the forest disappeared and sawmills closed, skilled hands that had once fashioned most of America's doors, windows, wagons and kitchen chairs were turned to the production of paper products in record volume. Other hands were retrained to create the world's largest aluminum cookware industry. Wisconsin has never feared change; it has capitalized on it.

More than any other central state, Wisconsin is likely to occupy the fantasies of Midwesterners, especially those from the prairies. Musing on visions of deep forests and aggressive game fish, they may well speak of it as not only beautiful but *different*. Probably this incomplete comparison is an unconscious recognition that between Western New York and the Black Hills, only Wisconsin offers to the eye a broken, varied skyline. It is not uncommon for a visitor to think of the state as mountainous though in fact elevation varies a scant 1,400 feet and Tim's Hill, the highest point, is less than 2,000 feet above sea level.

There may be a number of ways of dividing Wisconsin for purposes of description, but only one way seems self-evident. A relief map of the state immediately reveals physical divisions created by the advance and retreat of the great continental glacier. There is first the north country with its thousands of lakes, everything north of a line drawn from Chippewa Falls through Wausau to Oconto. This is country ground flat by the megatons of ice moving at a snail's pace. It is largely forest. To some, especially vacationers from distant states who come between Memorial Day and Labor Day, these woods *are* Wisconsin.

South of the woods is a broad, level plain between Lake Winnebago and the Wisconsin River. More specifically, it is defined by two glacial moraines, running roughly north and south on either side. Much of the plain is sandy; much of it is swampy. Some of it is good farm country; some supports industry. All of it is pretty.

Wisconsin's Lake Michigan shore is about 200 miles long. If you add the shoreline of Green Bay, the mileage comes to more than 300. Difficult as it may be to conceive, the big lake itself was created by the glacier as were all the Great Lakes. That's a lot of meltwater. Lake Michigan may be more important to the life of Wisconsin than any other single natural feature.

A trapezoidal section of South Central Wisconsin between Watertown and the Illinois border is dotted with small lakes and low hills of glacial drift known as drumlins. The contours of the land here have lent themselves to both dairy farming and tourism. It's a cultivated landscape, and some observers think that it is the prettiest part of the state. (That's a dangerous game to play in a place as richly endowed as Wisconsin). In the Wisconsin tradition of the balanced economy, the area supports its share of manufacturing at Beliot, Janesville, Madison, Watertown and Whitewater.

Curiously, the state may be better known for what the glacier failed to do than what it did to the land surface. The ice sheet never passed over the southwestern corner of the state. It is an area of curious rock formations and small, narrow valleys. It doesn't look at all like the Middle West of the popular imagination, but it's good farm country and projects an air of serenity that's hard to define.

How can such a panorama of natural and human riches as Wisconsin be captured in these few pages? It can't, of course, not wholly. Still, we hope that the photos and the text convey an honest, vivid and memorable impression of a state whose beauty and achievements need no exaggeration.

W.C.

Dairyland

In the census of 1870, only '25 Wisconsin farmers out of 160,000 identified themselves as dairymen. Most farmers grew wheat, an especially chancy crop and very hard on the soil. But during the following decade, the wheat farmers learned painfully that they could not compete against the yields from the prairies west of the Mississippi. Faced with ruin, they heeded the message of William Dempster Hoard, Wisconsin's advocate of dairy farming. What followed may be the most remarkable agricultural turnabout in the nation's history.

A native of dairy-rich New York, Hoard argued first in a weekly newspaper column, then later in his *Hoard's Dairyman*, that Wisconsin's farmers could no longer depend upon grain crops which depleted the soil. They should take up dairying, he said, for which the region, especially Southern Wisconsin, was ideally suited. Many farmers were convinced, especially among the newly arrived Scandinavians, Swiss, and Germans, who had brought with them at least some knowledge of dairy farming. Virtually starting from scratch, Wisconsin's new dairymen overtook New York in less than fifty years and displaced the Easterners as the country's top producers. Today, Wisconsin's license plates assure the world that it is still America's Dairyland.

Eight out of ten Wisconsin farmers are dairy farmers and the state produces more cheese than the other 49 combined. Dairying is common to every part of the state. But for reasons which may be largely romantic—the rolling terrain, the travel-poster landscape, the local color of ethnic communities like New Glaurus—South Central Wisconsin has captured the popular imagination as "Dairyland." And it was this region that pioneered Wisconsin's cheese-making, especially Green and Dane Counties.

Dairyland is drumlin country. The elongated, softly-contoured hillocks deposited by the glacier make great pasture and also provide scenery for painters and photographers. The uncomprising tidiness of this country, the small lakes and streams, the cultivation of woodlots—a legacy of the "oak openings" of the prairie days—combine to create an Arcadian atmosphere of settled prosperity.

Quaint New Glaurus, southwest of Madison in Green County, is the heart of what is lightly named Swissconsin. Here a combination of natural talent and shrewd, tasteful promotion exploit ethnic diversity in the name of tourism and cheese sales. The Swiss of New Glaurus were among the first to try making cheese in Wisconsin

(Preceding page) Water lilies and pickerelweeds enhance the shores of Laurel Lake.

(Left) Trilliums blanket the forest floor in springtime. This scene was captured in Door County.

(Below) A frozen waterfall, silenced by winter's chill, cascades silently from a sandstone cliff near LaCrosse.

(Opposite) The colors of late September are reflected in the peaceful waters of Drummond Lake, Bayfield County.

(Following pages) Golden aspens line the bluffs along the Mississippi in this autumnal view of Perrott State Park.

(Second following page, above) Morning mists rise from the water as a sailboat lies quietly at anchor in Green Bay.

(Second following page, below) Slabs of limestone form a narrow and rugged beach near Gills Rock, on the tip of the Door County Peninsula.

(Third following page) The serene Wisconsin River flows past a column of sandstone known as Chimney Rock, along the Upper Dells.

(Preceding pages) Snow-capped rocks cross this Northern Wisconsin stream like stepping-stones.

(Left) A bouquet of marsh marigolds springs from the mud of a country brook near Mt. Horeb.

(Below) A secluded lagoon is clothed in veils of mist as warm water meets the chilling air of a mid-September morning.

(Opposite) Broken slabs of brownstone form the irregular shoreline at Big Bay Point on Madelaine Island, in the Apostle chain.

(Following page) The attractive Norway Building is the focal point of the Norwegian-style buildings at Little Norway, near Blue Mounds. The building is modeled after a 12th-century Norwegian Church.

(Second following page, above) Billowing masses of cumulus clouds drift across the Mississippi River near Goose Island.

(Second following page, below) Jagged ice slabs, tipped on end and refrozen, are the result of an ice shove at Death's Door, near Gills Rock.

(Opposite) Driftwood bleaching in the sun is all that remains of a stand of trees that yielded to the fury of a Lake Superior storm in the Apostle Islands.

(Right) Sailboats lie at anchor in the protected waters of Sawyer Harbor, near Sturgeon Bay.

(Below) The shoreline of Cave Point becomes sheathed in ice from the far-reaching surf of Lake Michigan.

(Following page, above) The tranquil waters of Devils Lake reflect the passing summer clouds.

(Following page, below) The log barn and outbuilding were moved from Bayfield County to the Finnish farmstead at Old World Wisconsin, Eagle.

and they created a legend as well as an industry. Since the 1840s, they have continued to cultivate their old-country dress and customs. Tourists love it and they flock to the annual Wilhelm Tell and Heidi Festivals put on by the town. Between festivals, New Glaurus sells a lot of cheese. Other ethnic communities in Dairyland were quick to learn from the example of the Swiss. The Norwegian-Americans of Mt. Horeb in Dane County have also discovered fun and profit in sharing their Scandinavian traditions with visitors, and the handsome Norse church at Little Norway shows up on most tour itineraries.

Somewhat out of character, Dairyland encompasses one of the state's best known vacation areas, the little lake district around Lake Geneva in Walworth County. Since the mid-19th century, Geneva has been a fashionable summer resort for Chicagoans. It is now a popular winter playground as well. Before the Second World War, rising young business executives in Chicago aspired to ''a summer place at Geneva.'' For the status-conscious, it was a benchmark just beyond the acquisition of a home in Winnetka or River Forest.

Fashionable in its own way, nearby Lake Delavan claims the distinction of having served as winter headquarters for as many as 26 traveling circuses, including the famous P.T. Barnum troupe. Other Wisconsin towns have sheltered circuses in their time—Baraboo, Portage, Beaver Dam, Watertown, Janesville, Burlington, Evansville, Whitewater and tiny Wonewoc. The circus tradition is one of the most charming—and perhaps revealing—facets of the state's history. Even as far south as Delavan, winters are anything but mild. Why then would the ringmasters, acrobats, India Rubber Man and Tattooed Lady want to winter there? Possibly because a state that has always prided itself on its pluralism may be more hospitable, more downright friendly to the visitor who is different.

A much older touch of the exotic in Dairyland in Aztalan State Park near Lake Mills, east of Madison. It is a memorial to the 1837 discovery that the mysterious mounds of Southern Wisconsin were not natural features but man-made. Judge Nathaniel Hyer was the first to become aware of the pyramidal earthworks in Jefferson County, and decided that they must have been built by the Aztecs. He named the area Aztalan. It didn't take the 19th-century archaeologists long to conclude that the mounds were not the work of Aztecs. However, they made a wilder guess than Judge Hyer had. They claimed the Aztalan monuments, along with others, were effigy mounds in the form of animals and men, built by a mysterious and extinct race they called the Mound Builders.

(Preceding page) Autumn colors intensify the beauty of Eau Claire Dells, on the Eau Claire River near Hogarty.

At Kettle Moraine State Park near Whitewater, other more recent cultural monuments are being preserved at Old World Wisconsin Ethnic Village. On 500 acres within the Park, the State Historical Society is collecting and restoring buildings representative of the different ethnic groups settled in the state. Many will be farm houses, but there are also schools, town houses, and even a church. Old World Wisconsin is the only museum of its kind in the world, and a fitting monument to the state's ethnic past. When completed, the collection will represent more than 20 groups.

If you climb to the observation tower at the pinnacle of Blue Mounds near Mt. Horeb, you are at the highest point in southern Wisconsin, about 1,700 feet. On a fine summer's day, for 15 or 20 miles in any direction, the eye is treated to the soft green of sloping pasture, fields of corn, feed grass, and the dark green of trees. What you see may be the richest and most durable farm land in the country, so unmistakably dairy country that is it hard to conceive of its ever having been planted to wheat.

The Busy Lake Michigan Shore: Kenosha to Green Bay

Wisconsin is a big state, at some points 250 miles broad and 300 miles north to south. Unlike states which have tall mountains, deserts or malarial swamps, no corner of Wisconsin is truly uninhabitable or even markedly undesirable as a place to live. Nevertheless, more than half its people have chosen to live in a narrow corridor bordering Lake Michigan between the Illinois border and the base of Door Peninsula.

This concentration of people along the lakeshore is really not very mysterious. From the first days of European settlement, Michigan and the other Great Lakes provided ready communication and access to markets, first for agricultural products, later for manufactured goods as well. The lake was a source of food, too, although the lake fisheries have declined in importance in the past 50 years. The tempering effect of the lake on climate also drew settlers to its shores. A pedestrian on Milwaukee's

(Following page) Freezing rain and snow have silvered a hilltop forest near Blue Mounds, in Dane County.

East Wells Street, leaning into a January gale off the lake, might find this difficult to believe but meteoroligists assure us that it is so. Finally, there are aesthetics, a factor disregarded in geography tests. It is undeniably pleasant to live within easy access of an inland sea of fresh water.

Most visitors to Wisconsin probably come by car and the bulk of these are likely to enter the state by one of the major highways out of Chicago. Regardless of where he enters the state, the visitor may be interested to know that Wisconsin was the first to number its public highways for the convenience of motorists, an instance of that Wisconsin capacity to see the future coming and step out to meet it.

If the visitor driving north from Chicago is not in a hurry, he might wish to avoid heavily-traveled Interstate 94 and try Sheridan Road, closer to the lake. Enjoying frequent views of blue water on his right hand and finding the road bordered much of the way by well-kept lakeside parks, the traveler may be tempted to doubt the guidebook, which says that this is one of the country's major centers of heavy industry, specializing in motor vehicles and giant machinery. It is. In fact, the Kenosha-based American Motors Corporation is Wisconsin's largest employer.

The mainspring of the lakeside industrial corridor is, of course, the colorful metropolis of Milwaukee. Milwaukee is a city that most Americans like whether they have been there or not. It leads the country in the production of beer and motorcycles, enough in itself to win the town a place in the affections of any romantic of America's open road. The city also leads in the manufacture of padlocks, an activity which may symbolize that prudent foundation of the Milwaukee character which friends of the city would recognize. Underneath the *gemuetlichkeit* (geniality) of its national image—real enough in itself—is an old-world zest for hard work, frugality and getting ahead in life.

Milwaukee remains faithful to its promotional literature. It is a solid, family-based community, a heavily blue-collar community, a community long accustomed to, and demanding of, clean government. Appearing outwardly conservative, this city has many times elected and thrived under socialist mayors. It's a city that likes a good time but deplores rowdyism in any form. Milwaukee's tidy look and atmosphere of order never fail to make a good impression on visitors. The German flavor of the place—it was once called the German Athens because of the intellectual bent of its leaders—has been leavened since the turn of the century. The Polish, Italian and

(Preceding page, above) June brings lilacs and greenery to Cana Island lighthouse, located near Bailey's Harbor.
(Preceding page, below) Colorful daisies brighten this view of the Mississippi River at Perrot State Park,
Mt. Trempeleau looms behind.

Black communities within the city are now more visible in the life of the city. More than most American cities, Milwaukee has looked upon its ethnic enclaves as a source of strength and enrichment rather than of divisiveness.

Milwaukee remains Old Milwaukee in spirit, but the face of the city has changed noticeably since the end of the Second World War. Once rare, skyscrapers have given the downtown area a "modern" skyline, especially as viewed from the lake. Happily, the traditional light-colored brick is still much in evidence, especially in older residential neighborhoods, so that a traveler from a generation or two ago would have little doubt where he was. The legendary neighborhood taverns are still numerous and much frequented. Has anyone devised a more congenial place in which to unwind and kill a thirst on summer's afternoon after work lets out? And German restaurants, the good German restaurants, survive in Milwaukee, though increasingly they have had to share custom with Szechwanese, Greek, Peruvian, Polynesian and other more exotic cuisines.

Sociologists seem agreed that clever promotion of beer by Milwaukee's brewers has revolutionized national habits and made the six-pack as inseparable from television sports as hot dogs once were from circuses. Still, Milwaukee's lasting influence in the world is almost certainly in technology. In nations that have never seen a glass of beer, the typewriter—a Milwaukee invention—is indispensable to communication, education and even economic development. The impact on the world's future of another Milwaukee invention, the automated assembly line, cannot even be calculated. As a major producer of heavy industrial—machinery—tractors, earth-movers, turbines, diesel engines—Milwaukee is helping change the face of the Third World as it has already contributed to changing the face of ours.

Lake traffic in Milwaukee's small but busy harbor is a reminder that this port was once the gateway to Wisconsin, and, for many, to the New World. In the last century, most European, Canadian and even New England settlers coming to Wisconsin came not by Conestoga wagon but by lake steamer from Buffalo. The arrival of immigrant ships at Milwaukee has been described by John Muir, Hamlin Garland, and other Wisconsin writers whose families came this way. If you are imaginative, you may be able to recapture a bit of the flavor of this 19th-century adventure by sailing on the Chesapeake and Ohio ferries which still operate between Ludington, Michigan, and Milwaukee. There are few more pleasant excursions available today and surely no better way to comprehend the great size of Lake Michigan, this improbable creation of the Ice Age.

North of Milwaukee are the small industrial cities of Sheboygan, Manitowoc,

(Following pages) Autumn colors decorate the rock-bound Eau Claire River at Eau Claire Dells.

Two Rivers and Green Bay. Sheboygan has been in its brief history the country's largest manufacturer of kitchen chairs, and later, of glazed plumbing fixtures. Long a kind of model of the medium-sized American manufacturing towns, Sheboygan has known some difficult days in the last quarter century. Still, it remains neat, pleasant, and prosperous. Like many towns in Wisconsin, it is a major exporter of cheese.

The name of Manitowoc must have added an exotic note to German intelligence reports during the Second World War. No, the town was not sheltering spies; it was building submarines for the American Navy. They were sailed by way of Chicago's Drainage Canal and the Illinois River to the Mississippi and on to the sea. The Navy's decision was not a testimony to the security of the town's location but to the skill and versatility of its workers.

Neighboring Two Rivers also occupies a special niche in the history of American manufacturing as the birthplace of Wisconsin's important aluminum cookware industry. Neither the town nor the state had anything to recommend its entry into such an enterprise, except the mechanical aptitude and energy of its workers. Every ounce of aluminum had to be brought in from out of state. Magically, the industry spread—to Manitowoc, West Bend, Kewaunee and even to Eau Claire, across the state. Wisconsin now makes more aluminum cookware than all other states combined.

Green Bay is not on Lake Michigan proper but on a scenic 80-mile long inlet of the same name. It is the most famous city of 90,000 in North America. The Wisconsin state constitution was drafted here, but only a history buff is likely to remember that. It is also the place where the first European set foot on Wisconsin soil—Jean Nicolet, in 1634. Every school child has probably been told that but few remember. What we all remember is that this town is the home of the Green Bay Packers, one of the great professional football teams in history.

Like so many things in Wisconsin, the Packers, too, edge into that realm of paradox. Green Bay is the smallest metropolitan area with a National Football League franchise. It's also the oldest franchise in continuous operation. In this era of commercial giantism in sports, the successful team in the game has long been operated as a non-profit civic activity. To support their habit, the businessmen of Green Bay concern themselves with manufacturing paper, canning vegetables and processing cheese.

Extending northeast into Lake Michigan and forming the east shore of Green Bay is the rural and lovely Door Peninsula. Among both Wisconsites and visitors, Door is one of the best-loved areas of the state and the name generates pleasant associations of cherry orchards, picturesque country lanes bordered by stone fences, undisturbed rocky shores and artists' colonies. Door enjoys an atmosphere of remoteness out of proportion to the scant hundred miles from metropolitan Milwaukee which the map shows.

Door once held an important place in Lake Michigan fisheries, especially Sturgeon Bay where, legend has it, the sturgeon used to be stacked on shore like cordwood. Washington Island, off the tip of the Peninsula, has won a permanent place in the guidebooks as the earliest Icelandic community in America.

The Driftless Southwest

When the continental glacier moved southward to cover most of North America in the last Ice Age, it separated into two giant lobes somewhere in the vicinity of present-day Eau Claire, leaving untouched an area of about 15 thousand square miles of what is Southwestern Wisconsin and narrow strips of Minnesota and Iowa. This unglaciated or ''driftless'' area—drift is the rubble of the glacier (stones, gravel, sand)—is unique in North America and gives us an idea what the Middle West probably looked like before the Ice Age.

Part of the fascination of the driftless area lies in its curiously broken terrain, country that was never ground flat by the weight of the mile-high ice sheet. Around Camp Douglas the breaks in the skyline are sometimes sharp and angular and bring to mind the familiar rock formations of the American West, memorialized in cowboy movies. There is no comparable landscape east of the Mississippi. Further west on I-90 the landscape is not only more ''normal,'' but remarkably pretty. It softens dramatically into a country of rolling wooded hillsides and lush small valleys, some dead-ending unexpectedly like the box canyons of the Far West. This is the famous coulee country, a region described by Hamlin Garland in his Middle Border books with a kind of awe. Garland was born at Onalaska on the Mississippi and spent his early years on a farm in Green's Coulee, not far from the La Crosse River. With the naive sexism of his era, he recollects the coulee as ''a delightful place for boys'' to grow up.

(Following page, above) A circular bed of tulips adorns the approach to the State Capitol Building in Madison.
(Following page, below) Early-morning fog begins to lift above the valley farms near Arcadia in Trempeleau County.

Endowed with unique natural features and an almost exotic beauty, the driftless area is denied what may be the most common feature of the Wisconsin countryside—an abundance of lakes. Since the glacier did not pass this way, it left no scoured lake bottoms nor melt-water to fill them. Man-made lakes are few, and natural lakes exceedingly rare, like Devil's Lake, one of Wisconsin's most popular. Devil's Lake, at the edge of the driftless area in the Baraboo Range, occupies the pre-glacial stream bed of the Wisconsin River. The ends of the lake are "plugged" with debris which the glacier pushed ahead of it. Despite its creation from nature's odds and ends, and contrary to its uncomplimentary name, Devil's Lake is a beauty. Its deep blue water is bordered on almost all sides by steep wooded bluffs and frequent outcropping of rock, popular spots for hikers to sun themselves. At sunset, the quartzite cliffs often glow with unforgettable shades of red, pink, and lavender. Natural or not, Devil's could scarcely seem more unlike the typical lake of Wisconsin's North Woods.

The driftless Southwest is Wisconsin's oldest settled area. The first territorial capital was at Leslie in Lafayette County, due to the discovery of lead—"mineral" as it was called. This first attracted white settlers in large numbers to the territory. The Mississippi provided the most convenient route. In the 1820s thousands of American southerners came up the river to try their luck at mining. The shallow surface mines scraped by these early miners are said to have caused a long-forgotten observer to liken them to so many "badger holes," and very soon Wisconsites were known as "badgers." The miners from the South were joined in time by others, first New England Yankees, later experienced miners from Cornwall and Wales. Mineral Point in the heart of the mine country became not only the most important town in the territory, but also the largest settlement of Cornishmen in America.

Some of the charm of this early Cornish settlement is preserved in the quaint stone cottages on Shake Rag Street. Built of limestone quarried close by, the houses are modeled after the early miners' traditional homes back in Cornwall. The name Shake Rag Street also preserves a local Cornish tradition: the Hammills, the Chenoweths, the Pendarvises, Trebilcocks and other "Cousin Jacks," as the Cornishmen where known, were summoned to dinner from the hillside mines by their wives signaling with kitchen towels. Gone from Mineral Point are the "kiddly-winks," Cornish taverns where miners could relax over a pint of ale, but Cornish pastries and saffron buns are still delicious local traditions.

A descendant of early Welsh settlers and worshipful son of the Wisconsin countryside was the architect Frank Lloyd Wright, born at Richland Springs. Wright

(Preceding page) Veins of foam on the river's face are the aftermath of the turbulent St. Croix Falls at Interstate Park.

38

never escaped the powerful spell of the country drained by the lower Wisconsin River, its fertile fields, its narrow green valleys, its enchanting rock formations. For his own permanent home, Taliesin—now an architectural shrine—he chose a hillside in the village of Spring Green and gathered his materials locally, especially stone. Wright said that a house should seem to have "grown out of the countryside," and Taliesin, named for an ancient Welsh bard, exemplifies this principle. The low stone house is so much a part of the landscape that it is said to disappear from view when weather conditions reduce visibility. A tempestuous genius, Frank Lloyd Wright was given to disputes with his Wisconsin neighbors and spent much of his later life in self-imposed "exile." But when he died, his body was brought back to his beloved state for burial at Unity Chapel in the Wyoming Valley, the first building he had a hand in designing.

Up river from Frank Lloyd Wright country, at the great bend in Wisconsin, is Wisconsin Dells, a tourist attraction since 1880. The Dells, like so many curious natural features, can be attributed to the glacier. When the ice sheet blocked the old course of the river, the water cut a new channel through these soft sandstone cliffs, creating a region of outlandish and fascinating rock formations, given broadly descriptive name like Devil's Elbow, Grand Piano, and Great Arrowhead. A visitor can best appreciate the Dells from the level of the river, especially on a warm and sunny summer day, when the water is low and quiet and the excursion boats move slowly among the strange red rocks.

The town of Baraboo, a few miles south of the Dells, has become the Cooperstown of the American circus. In the 1880s, after the state's circus tradition had already taken root at Delavan, five sons of August Ringling, a German-born harness maker in Baraboo, organized a family circus and took it on the road. After some experimenting with names, they settled on the Ringling Brothers Circus and by 1888 the family show had grown to a traveling company that required 30 railroad cars. In 1907, the Ringlings bought out the widow of their competitor, P.T. Barnum, and became in truth, "the Greatest Show on Earth." For 34 years the Ringlings brought their performers and animals back to Baraboo to spend the winter. In 1918, for the last time, the troupe left the old brick and stone winter quarters in Wisconsin, and in time they made the inevitable move to the winter sunshine of Florida. Visitors to Baraboo today will find the American circus tradition still alive and well at Circus World Museum, operated since 1959 by the State Historical Society. The stables that sheltered elephants and lions in the last century now house circus exhibits. In

(Following page, above) The roof of Swallow's Nest juts out over the frozen Wisconsin River, while High Rock and Romance Cliff form the jaws of the Upper Dells at Wisconsin Dells.
(Following page, below) Purple loosestrife surrounds the quiet waters of Shadow Lake, in Waupaca.

(Preceding page) Shore-to-shore water lilies cover this small lake near Amery, in Polk County.

(Left) Large-leafed asters carpet the woods and clearings at Rock Island Park in August.

(Below) A peninsula of colorful maples is reflected in a sheltered cove on Bass Lake.

(Opposite) The setting winter sun imparts scant warmth to Wisconsin's woods and lakes.

(Following pages) A sprinkle of mountain ash heightens the autumn color along the shores of Devil's Island.

(Second following page) The freezing surf of Lake Michigan forms attractive ice formations at Cave Point Park near Valmy.

(Preceding page, above) The sun's last rays touch the surface of Green Bay, rippled by the evening breeze, at Fish Creek.

(Preceding page, below) The long-stalked purple blazing star is a native prairie wild-flower.

(Left) The Galloway House, in Fond du Lac, is operated by a local historical society as a museum site.

(Following page, above) Bass Lake reflects the bright colors of autumn.

(Following page, below) Potatatomi Light-house, erected in 1836 on Rock Island, is the oldest light in Wisconsin. Rock Island is now a state park.

(Second following page) Limestone cliffs loom like fortress walls above the waters of Lake Michigan.

(Opposite) Tamaracks and red grass border the swales at the Ridges Sanctuary, where a variegated landscape provides interesting nature trails.

(Right) The lighted dome of the State Capitol dominates Madison's nighttime skyline.

(Below) Sherwood Point Lighthouse is closed for the season as ice entirely covers Green Bay.

(Following page) Reds and golds of autumn highlight the shores of Tamarack Lake, in Oneida County.

(Second following page, above) Early morning clouds appear inverted in the still surface of Lake Watersmeet, near Eagle River.

(Second following page, below) Gibraltar Rock, near Lodi, offers this pastoral view from its summit.

(Third following page, above) Late afternoon sun lights up the water-sculpted Sugar Bowl and Grotto Rock, of the Lower Dells on the Wisconsin River.

(Third following page, below) Evening sun wanes over Eagle Harbor, a sheltered cove at Ephraim, where sailboats anchor for the night.

summer, visiting circus stars perform in the Museum's tent exhibit, keeping fresh the spirit of ''the big top.''

Despite its early date of settlement, the driftless area has remained essentially agrarian and the towns small. Prarie du Chien, the second oldest European settlement in the state, still has fewer than seven thousand residents; La Crosse, the only city in the Southwest, about 50 thousand. Dairy farms are numerous, as they are everywhere in Wisconsin, but so are grain fields, especially corn. And in spring, apple blossoms bring an extra touch of beauty to such already well-favored country as the Kickapoo Valley.

This quiet Southwest is historic country. In June, 1673, the explorers Marquette and Jolliet drifted down the last few miles of the Wisconsin to the Mississippi, the imperial waterway of North America. The general success of the French mission into the Mississippi Valley has often been attributed to Father Marquette's kindly treatment of the Indians. By contrast, it was across this same country a century and a half later in the summer of 1832 that Chief Black Hawk fled the wrath of the white man. The tiny town of Victory on State Highway 35 overlooking the Mississippi is thought to mark the site of the Battle of Bad Axe, where Black Hawk suffered final defeat in the last major Indian revolt east of the river.

Perhaps because of the extent and commercial importance of Wisconsin's Great Lakes' shorelines, we tend to forget that it is a Mississippi River state, too. Its 200-mile river border—not much less than Arkansas'—has only one port of any size, La Crosse, and Wisconsin's banks are more likely to be noted for their natural beauty than for their commercial importance. Some of the river bluffs rise to 500 feet above the stream, especially around Alma. The view from here has few equals. William Cullen Bryant, in fact, ranked these river bluffs in majesty with anything he had seen on the Rhine or Danube. He added that ''this place should be visited by every poet and painter in America.'' This is certainly easy to agree with.

Between the Moraines

Moraine is a geologist's word, meaning a ridge of earth and loose stones piled up by the advance of the continental ice sheet. There are several kinds of moraine and Wisconsin is rich in all of them, as in most glacial phenomena. That's why the last period of the Ice Age has been named the Wisconsin Stage. Moraines in

(Preceding page) Garden-variety lilies enhance the picturesque Sherwood Point Lighthouse near Sturgeon Bay.

Wisconsin are extensive enough to serve as markers for whole large areas of the state and important enough to be protected by state law, some just for uses of science, others for sight-seeing and recreation. The new "Ice Age Trail" will provide hiking and bicycle trails along the ridge of the great terminal moraine which runs through the center of the state and marks the bounds of the driftless area. The longest portion begins roughly south of Langlade County, passes Madison on the west, then hooks sharply southeast toward Janesville.

In the eastern part of the state, running between Lake Michigan and Winnebago, is another kind of moraine, rather a course of moraines called "kettles." A kettle is characterized by a pond or a depression at its ridge-line, formed by the melt-water from giant chunks of ice dropped by the glacier. The kettle line has been much altered by human activity, but two stretches are being preserved at Kettle Moraine State Forest north of West Bend and at Kettle Moraine State Park between Waukesha and Janesville.

Between the two moraines lies the central plain of Wisconsin, a region whose symbiotic mix of farming, manufacturing, hardwood forests, wildlife preserves and recreation areas comes close to representing the Wisconsin ideal of balanced civilization. The receding glacier and its melt-water have left this a watery domain, a soft, spongy country, full of lakes, swamps of marshy woodlands, slow waterways, and sand, whole counties of it. It's a place where water birds, cranberries, and vegetables thrive, where cows can produce record yields of milk from grazing in low-lying pastures. To many thoughtful observers, it is the real heart of Wisconsin.

Unlike the situation in the southern part of the state, where rich and fruitful farms lie close to one another, here on the wet and sandy plain, wilderness demands—and gets—its share of elbow room by refusing to support agriculture except on its own terms. Many efforts have been made to drain the marshes and use the land for conventional farming. Almost inevitably they fail, but men keep trying. One such experiment earlier in this century ended ironically with the state's requesting Federal assistance in reflooding the land. The extensive wetlands notwithstanding, the plain is rich in agriculture, especially in dairying and the growing of vegetables for canning.

It was to this farm country in the Wisconsin heartland that the naturalist John Muir was brought from Scotland as a boy of eleven. He credited the countryside, around the family farm near Ennis Lake in Marquette County, with awakening in him that profound response to nature which was to make him America's voice of conservation. "Here without knowing it we were still at school," he writes in his

(Following page) Early morning sunlight touches pines and sedges with a rosy glow.

memoirs of his arrival in America; "every wild lesson a love lesson not whipped but charmed into us. Oh, that glorious Wisconsin wilderness! . . . Young hearts, young leaves, flowers, animals, the winds and the streams and the sparkling lake, all wildly, gladly rejoicing together!"

In the northeast corner of the plain, Lake Winnebago is a classic Wisconsin paradox. Thirty miles long by ten wide, Winnebago is one of the largest natural lakes in America. It is also one of the shallowest with a maximum depth of just 21 feet, like a platter into which someone has poured a glass of water. For all its modest volume, however, it serves the surrounding communities well both in industry and recreation. In winter it becomes a paradise for iceboaters, offering a 200-square mile expanse, which freezes fast and stays frozen.

The east and west shores of Winnebago present a contrast. Much of the west shore is lined by industrial cities and towns; the east shore, bordered for most of its length by the Niagara cuesta, a picturesque rocky promontory, is one of the most scenic areas in Wisconsin. There is no town of greater than a few hundred in population along its length. At the north end of the lake is one of the world's most important centers of paper manufacture, the Appleton-Neenah-Menasha urban complex. This industry expanded in the wake of the cutting-over of Wisconsin's original forests and has made ingenius use of the once despised aspen and other scrub trees of the second growth. There's hardly a better illustration of making a virtue of necessity. In addition to prospering wonderfully, the Wisconsin pulp and paper industry has established a fine record of public concern. Their investment of more than 50 million dollars in pollution prevention has much to do with Wisconsin's water tasting purer now than it did more than a century ago.

Appleton has done more than make paper products. Here in 1882, the country's first hydroelectric generator was brought on line. And a spinoff from this pioneer power plant was the installation of America's first permanent electric streetcar line. Appleton was the hometown of the late Senator Joe McCarthy. It was also the hometown of novelist Edna Ferber, whose family had fled antisemitic persecution in a neighboring state. The fugitive Ferbers were warmly welcomed in Appleton, remembered by Edna as a "tree shaded, prosperous, civilized place."

Down Winnebago's west shore from Appleton, at the mouth of the Wolf River, is Oshkosh, a town whose name often draws smiles and triggers associations of Frank Grove's bib overalls. Named for a Menominee Chief, Oshkosh has long been an

(Preceding page, above) Columns of oat shocks dot the rolling fields near LaCrosse.
(Preceding page, below) Precariously perched on its tilted base, this ten-foot block of granite rests high above Devils Lake, at Devils Lake State Park near Baraboo.

important small industrial city and once led the nation in production of doors, windows, carriages, wagons and matches. That's quite a record for a town which still has fewer than 55 thousand people.

Just 25 miles west of shallow Winnebago is Green Lake, Wisconsin's deepest. At some points it reaches a depth of 235 feet, deeper than Lake Erie. Tourists may be assured that the lake is actually a dark green. Like Geneva, Green is a very pretty lake with steep wooded shores. Close to Green Lake is the charming little college town of Ripon. It claims to be the birthplace of the Republican party, but the claim is disputed by others, notably Jackson, Michigan. However almanac editors decide such matters, it is certainly true that men who were to become influential in the party met here at Ripon in 1854 to discuss formation of an anti-slavery party. Whatever the case, Ripon is the kind of picture postcard American town that any organization would be proud to claim as its birthplace.

The little town of Clintonville, about half way between Appleton and Wausau, illustrates beautifully that Wisconsin tradition of mechanical and industrial know-how showing up in the unexpected place. Located in the middle of a large and prosperous farming area, this town of five thousand is the birthplace of the four-wheel-drive vehicle. In 1900, two local machinists, William Besserich and Otto Zachow "fiddled around" until they had produced such a vehicle and then established the FWD plant to produce it. Almost 80 years later, the FWD plant is still doing business in Clintonville.

Well upstream on the Wisconsin River is Wausau, a model of how "the good life" may perhaps be best achieved in an industrial town of about 50 thousand. Thanks to a local insurance company, and its advertising campaigns, Wausau may have the most familiar railroad depot in the country. A disinterested observer would surely concede that both depot and town come close to what the late Norman Rockwell used to see in his fantasies when he stood before his drawing board.

The North Woods And The Lake Superior Highland

Back in the 1930s, Mr. Bailey, the kindly, tuft-eared boss in Walter Berndt's *Chicago Tribune* comic strip, *Smitty*, used to cushion himself against the

discomforts of a prairie winter by daydreaming of his summer vacation in the "North Woods."

As he nodded in his office swivel chair, he pictured himself in fishing togs, seated in a rowboat with his toothy Indian guide, George, as they angled for the wily giant muskellunge, "Old Fighter." In Mr. Bailey's idiom—and that of most prairie dwellers—"the North Woods" could only mean Wisconsin. If he had meant the Michigan woods or the Minnesota woods, he would have said just that.

A look at a map of Northern Wisconsin should reveal at once how the North Woods became synonymous with game fishing. It looks as though someone had been swinging a paint brush loaded with light-blue ink. Thousand of lakes—some claim Wisconsin has more than ten thousand—fill the map from the Nicolet National Forest on the east to the St. Croix River on the west. Mapped and unmapped, the lakes vary in size from less than an acre to the generous expanses of Lac du Flambeau or Court d'Oreilles. Wisconsin's North Woods shelters one of the three or four greatest concentrations of lakes in the world.

Like so many natural features in the state, the northern lakes are a legacy of the glacier. The ice sheet first scoured out thousands of natural basins and then deposited detritus to act as dams for the melt-water. So numerous are the lakes that a motorist traveling Highway 70 from Grantsburg to Florence will rarely find himself out of sight of blue water. Even when seen from the air, at altitudes up to 8,000 feet, the country appears to be a limitless and irregular pattern of dark green and blue. This view from the air discourages any temptation to challenge Rhinelander's claim that there are 230 lakes within 12 miles of its town center.

The departure of the loggers for the Far West and the appearance of a second growth woodland ushered in the age of recreation in the North Woods. In the early years recreation meant game fishing, especially the pursuit of the powerful muskie. Quickened by reports of 60 pounders being taken from the lakes around Hayward, summer tourism grew into a significant source of income for an area that history appeared to have left behind. The Soo Line and Milwaukee Road began to run "fishermen's specials" in the summer.

Winter in the North Woods was another story. There was a time when the end of Labor Day Weekend saw a seasonal quiet settling over the woods. The sparse population of year-round residents would begin to lay in a supply of firewood. Hibernating animals would shuffle through the falling leaves searching out an adequate hole or tree hollow. That has changed. Now Labor Day is a signal that things are just about to liven up. What made the difference was the roar of the first

(Preceding pages) Cirrus clouds enshroud the setting sun over the Mississippi River at Alma.

66

snowmobile in the early 1960s. It turned not only the North Woods, but also the state into a major winter vacation area.

The refinements of year-round tourism tend to obscure the rough and turbulent past of the north country. In those days many Wisconsin farmers would leave home after the harvest to join the career loggers for a long winter of cutting in "the pineries." The isolated, unnatural masculine world brought communities designed, it seemed, as arenas of violence. An old North Woods boast was that "the four toughest places in creation are Cumberland, Hayward, Hurley and Hell." A footnote cautioned that of the four, Hurley was the toughest.

Wisconsin has passed through an age of reckless and extravagant use of its forests. What was done in the last century cannot be undone, of course, but today Wisconsites and all who love the state can take comfort in the fact that the new growth is being managed with all the skill known to modern forestry, much of it in two vast National Forests, the Chequamegon and the Nicolet. Almost more important than the economic function of the woods is that they satisfy an ancient need in man for the cover of trees and communion with wildlife. It doesn't much matter whether this is second, third or even subsequent growth. The yearning is for trees, water, and the sounds of nature. These are still abundant, even in an age of power boats and snowmobiles.

While the saw and the axe were new to Wisconsin's woods in the 19th century, fire was not. Conservationist and forester Aldo Leopold tells us that for 20 thousand years there has been a struggle for living space between prairie grass and trees with fire as the weapon. He writes that thousands of years ago the woods were ravaged by fires to such an extent that the edge of the prairie was pushed almost to Lake Superior. Curiously, it has been the action of European man turning the prairies of Southern Wisconsin into farms and woodlots that has curbed the fires in our century, and tipped the balance in favor of the woods.

If the traveler continues north on US 51 or Wisconsin 13, he will in time leave the woods behind and enter the Lake Superior area. The clearings along the way show evidence of red clay and ferrous soil. This is old mining country. It is also a land of blueberries and, further on, orchards of pears and apples. From an occasional rise in the highway, the driver may catch that first startling view of the unique blue of Lake Superior in the near distance.

The only term for Lake Superior is awesome. It is the world's largest body of

(Following page, above) A panoramic view of the Wisconsin River valley can be seen from Gibraltar Rock near Lodi.
(Following page, below) The serene Milwaukee River winds its way through Milwaukee, the beer capitol of America.

fresh water and looks it. Superior's volume equals that of all the other Great Lakes combined with three extra Eries thrown in. There is a local saying that if you drown in the lake, your body will never surface. This appears to be a romantic way of saying that the water is cold. This is an understatement. As a matter of record many persons have drowned and many ships have gone down in its icy waters. For all its beauty, this lake can be scary.

The wind blows a lot around Lake Superior and when it does the surf can pound the shore with all the authority of an ocean. In the depth of winter, the lake freezes over for a couple of months. Before that its spray is likely to cover everything along its shores with several inches of ice. It makes for lovely picture postcards, but is hard on the nose and ears. In summer, of course, the cool atmosphere of the lake can be a heavenly sanctuary for vacationers from the steaming cities of the midlands.

Lake Superior scenery is epitomized and happily preserved in the Apostle Islands National Seashore off the tip of Bayfield Peninsula. The Islands were named by an unknown French fur-trader. It's hard to say whether he was weak in arithmetic, scripture, or just eyesight. There are actually twenty-two islands in the group. Three centuries ago the Apostles lay at the busy crossroads of the fur trade. Today the islands are a preserve of low, quiet woods, red cliffs rising sharply from the water, solitary coves and caves, and broad tawny beaches spotted with driftwood. Wave action against the sandstone cliffs has created arches and rock formations which rival the driftwood in their curious shapes.

Fifty miles to the west of the Apostles, at the far corner of the lake, is the city of Superior, one of the country's great ports. Were it not for winter ice the volume of shipping from Superior might equal in tonnage that of East Coast seaports like Baltimore. Rising, as it seems to, right out of the sand flats, Superior presents a haunting image when viewed from the east along the lake shore. This impression seems to be strengthened by the way its Great Northern ore docks and the grain elevators break into the pale northern sky.

Not far south of Superior is the source of one of Wisconsin's most picturesque and beloved rivers, the St. Croix. At St. Croix Falls, the river has cut a 200-foot gorge through the pre-Cambrian basalt. Called The Dalles, a French cognate of English dells, the spectacular stretch of rock cliffs, rapids, and giant potholes is maintained by Wisconsin and Minnesota in the unusual Interstate State Park.

(Preceding page) Snow-clad pines stand like sentinels over this quiet retreat at White Sand Lake.

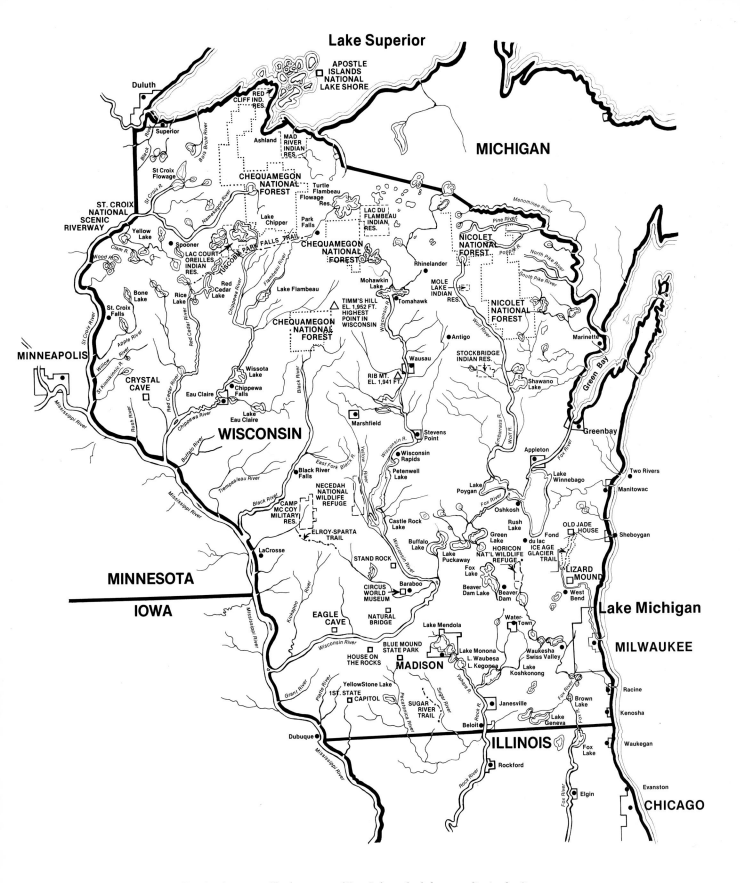

(Following page) Evening breezes ruffle the waters of Post Lake as day's last rays dim in the distance.